Charles & Kath Bartlam

Photographers of Court Street, Madeley

Charles & Kath Bartlam

Photographers of Court Street, Madeley

by

Alan J. Heighway & Peter Wilson

Logaston Press

LOGASTON PRESS
Little Logaston, Logaston,
Woonton, Almeley, Herefordshire HR3 6QH
www.logastonpress.co.uk

First published by Logaston Press 2010
Copyright © Alan J. Heighway 2010

ISBN 978 1 906663 39 1

Typeset by Logaston Press
and printed in Great Britain by
Bell & Bain Ltd., Glasgow

*This book is dedicated to
Alma and Archie Heighway*

Author details

Alan Heighway from Madeley and wife Barbara (née Smitherman) from Wellington have always had an interest in both local and Shropshire history. Alan was educated at Madeley Infants school, then the junior school opposite St Michael's church, on to Madeley Modern and finally at Wellington Technical College where he qualified as a Mechanical Engineering Technician. Alan and Barb met at a dance at the Majestic in Wellington and both worked at Ever Ready Dawley, until getting married at Christ Church Wellington in 1967 when they moved to an old cottage in Dark Lane, Dawley. Two years later they moved to West Street, St Georges, where they had two children Helen and Brett, and have lived there ever  since. Alan and Barb were also local photographers for around 30 years known as 'Telford Photo Services' working as resident photographers at dinner dances and taking pictures of stars appearing at the great old Forest Glen by the Wrekin, Terry Heath's Town House at Wellington, and also at Oakengates Town Hall (now The Place). Alan was also a freelance press photographer and, for four years was the chairman of the 'Wrekin Arts Photographic Club'. Since having his first camera at the age of 12, Alan has collected all types of old classic cameras and now has over 1,500 in his collection, which also includes photographs, postcards and various photographic memorabilia. Alan and Barb often give talks to local clubs and residential homes about the cameras in between their activities as line dance teachers.

Peter Wilson was born in Madeley and has always taken an interest in local history, his great grandfather having owned the Tontine Hotel. He believes that photographs of both buildings and people, are a valuable visual record that can be referred to in the future. After Alan had said he had a few negatives that he wished Peter to scan and put onto a CD, Peter thought he had a small job ahead of him, until he saw the suitcase that Alan brought over. Two and a half to three years soon passed by but Peter feels that all the work was worth it as the Bartlam collection will stay in the archives forever together with the names of the people identified.

Contents

Authors' Acknowledgements

Many people have helped in the identification of the images and particular thanks are due to the following: Mark Amess, Barbara Ashton, Avril Axon, Della Bailey, Doreen Banks, Jane Biggs, Linda Boddison, John & Kay Booth, Rose Bridgwater, Ian Bullock, Helen Carline, Jan Cockerill, Cis Cowdell, Ron & Jill Colley, Tom Cookson, Eileen Corbett, Liz Davies (Wilkes), Shirley Davies, Shelby Dawson, Malcolm Dearing, Janet Doody, Sharon Evans, Stella Ferrington (Burgess), Graham Foster, Hilary Fowler, Ron France, Eric Frost, Judith Fulerem, Michael Guy, Michael Anthony Guy, Pat Hakanson, Ernie Hardman, Sharon Harris, Yvonne Harris, Kenny Harrison, Phil Haseley, Sam Haseley, Alma Heighway, Gordon Heighway, Sue Hemming (Fletcher), Margaret Hicks, Molly Higginson, Paul Hill, Bill Hodgkiss, Pat Howlett, Sheila & Terry Humphries, Mike Jardine, Keith Jenkinson, Alan T. Jones, Jean Jones, Shirley Jones, Martin Lansche, Beryl Lloyd, Tina Marshall, Toby Neal, Margaret Owen, Wendy Palin, Judith Pankhurst, Doreen Parton, Margaret Perks, Sambrook family, Mrs Shepherd, Vera Skitt, Mike Tait, Eileen Taylor (Sambrook), Joyce Taylor, Cathy Thompson, Betty Tommy, Ann Vaughan, Rob Walton, Jennifer Waters, Sarah Williams, Simon Wilde, Iris Workman – and a special thanks to Peter Wilson's wife Jen who helped with the work.

Sincere apologies to anyone we have omitted!

Disclaimer

We have done our best to ensure that the identifications are correct and that all names are spelled correctly – however, in some cases, we have been given conflicting information and, where errors have crept in, we apologise unreservedly. Please let us know if you spot any errors by contacting shelagh@madeleyparishcouncil.gov.uk.

Preface

The Bartlam Photographic Studio operated from premises in Court Street, Madeley for around 40 years. During that time Charles and Kath Bartlam took thousands of photographs of local people as well as a small number of scenes and events. Unfortunately, many of the originals have been lost or destroyed over the years but around 2,500 negatives were recovered thanks to the authors of this book and Christopher Bartlam. An Awards for All grant, obtained by the Madeley Living History Project, facilitated the digitisation of the images by Nathaniel Stevenson (Shropshire Archives Reprographics Officer) as well as the publication of this volume and the commissioning of a headstone for the previously unmarked grave in St. Michael's churchyard, Madeley, where the Bartlams are buried.

No studio records survived, apart from the negatives, and a mammoth task was undertaken to try to identify as many of the subjects as possible. This was carried out via displays, talks and a temporary website as well as appeals in the local and regional press.

Around 600 of the negatives have now been identified and they are all included in the following pages. In the main, Studio Photographs section the photographs have been arranged broadly in alphabetical order by surname (and married names in the case of women), except where it has been necessary to amend the order so as to allow multiple portraits of one person to appear on the same page, as far as is possible. The index lists all those included (by maiden and married name in the case of many of the women). We very much hope that a substantial proportion of the remaining photographs will be named in years to come so that further volumes can be produced.

The original negatives have now been deposited at Shropshire Archives and grateful thanks are due to the staff there, especially Nat Stevenson, for all their help with this project. Thanks are also due to the many people who have assisted with the project in various ways particularly the Madeley History Group who have been tireless in their efforts to put names to faces. Last, but by no means least, I would like to thank Alan and Pete for bringing this collection to my attention in the first place. It has been a pleasure to help with a project of such significance for the people of Madeley.

Shelagh Lewis
Madeley Living History Project
Madeley Parish Council
July 2010

Charles and Kath Bartlam – an appreciation

It seems strange that I should be paying a tribute to somebody that I never knew or ever had the chance to meet, but I feel passionately that Charles Bartlam, the Madeley photographer, should be classed alongside the many past 'Shropshire Born and Bred' great sons of our fantastic county.

Charles Bartlam was born in 1876 at Madeley Wood, between Madeley and Ironbridge. At the age of four he was orphaned but remained living in the area looked after by local families.

Kathleen & Charles Bartlam

By the time he was a young man in his early twenties, he was living in lodgings in Court Street, Madeley, and it appears that he spent the rest of his life in 72 Court Street until his death at the age of 63 in 1939. He was known as a respected and competent motor car mechanic, and played music in local brass bands, but it was in photography that he excelled and became a craftsman. Around 1905 he opened his Photographic & Artistic Studio at his home and this was to become the centre point for all the prolific Bartlam work that followed.

Charles Bartlam outside 72 Court Street

I do not know how Charles met his future wife (my Great Aunty Kathleen Watts from Uttoxeter, near Stoke) but what is certain is that she joined him at Court Street after their marriage at St Michael's Church, Madeley on 29 December 1914.

Kathleen Bartlam outside 72 Court Street

Under his guidance she also became a competent craftsman in the art of photography, even continuing to keep the studio open for a further nine years after Charles's death until around 1948, giving a studio time span totalling over 40 years. Kath also became a master at re-touching negatives using special pencils, and on many of the negatives you can see the places where re-touching has occurred. Colour photography was not available to them and she also developed a gift for adding colour and tinting black & white pictures with dyes to provide a new dimension to the images, or they were sepia toned to great effect. Many of these sepia and colour tinted pictures are still on display in Madeley homes today, and I have a couple of examples in my own collection.

This must have been a very active period for the Bartlams, and other photographers like them, as not only did the sittings have to be pre-arranged, but the production of the final

Four studio portraits of Kathleen Bartlam

photograph must also have taken a considerable amount of time. The film plates had to be loaded and prepared before exposure, the sittings completed and the exposed plates removed and developed. They would have needed to employ contact printing frames for each print, using a piece of unexposed photographic paper and the developed negative clamped together. Each one would have to be given a timed exposure to daylight (later to an electric lightbulb), as a lighting source, as they did not have an enlarger as far as I am aware. Washing and drying both prints and negatives must have been a challenge as all this took place in a tin shed workshop and darkroom at the side of the house. Chemicals were not so user friendly in those days and the Bartlams would be working in these conditions for many hours every week throughout the year.

Kathleen Bartlam

Thornton Pickard brass and mahogany plate cameras with brass lenses were used in the early days (although Aunty Kath later sold these), and most of the few glass plates saved must have been taken with this equipment. However, as camera development progressed, they purchased and used a Kodak 'post card' size negative camera for most of the 2500 portraits saved.

All of Kath Bartlam's work would have been taken with such a camera. A Bartlam Kodak folding camera and the Bartlam rubber stamp were found with the negatives in the old shop. They have been cleaned up and are now in my Classic Camera Collection.

Charles Bartlam and the 'Pig on the wall' postcard

There is a lot of Shropshire mist surrounding this very famous postcard, but there is no doubt in my mind that Charles Bartlam was involved in its creation in his early days. Christopher Bartlam has confirmed that the original version was altered by Charles in the workshop at Court Street following a court case, and that he altered and then produced and re-printed the postcard from there. Aunty Kath also confirmed to me that this was the case. There is also no doubt in my mind that the original glass plate for the main picture of the 'Man and Pig' was taken by one of the Baldwin Brothers of Dawley and, at the time of the postcard's creation, Charles Bartlam was a partner in the joint photographic company that was called 'Baldwin Brothers and Bartlam' with studios at both

Who was it that put the pig on the wall to see Captain Webb's procession pass?

In August 1875 Captain Matthew Webb from Dawley became the first man to swim the English Channel, but it was it was to be 1909 before a commemorative postcard was made, to coincide with a monument erected in Dawley High Street to mark the event. The now famous 'Baldwin Brothers and Bartlam' 'Pig on the Wall' postcard was born, the top picture being a remake. After complaints from publican Ernst Fletcher, the man featured, Charles Bartlam was taken to court for not having his permission to use his image before selling the postcard in public. He lost the case and was fined, but asked the judge for permission to alter the features of the publican, which he did at the Court Street studio, the result being the image on the left that is well known today

Madeley and Dawley. At some stage there must have been a separation of the partnership and it would seem fair to say that 'Pig on the wall' postcards with both names printed on it would be the earlier versions, and that those bearing the attribution 'Charles Bartlam – Madeley Salop' are the ones printed by him in Madeley.

Bartlam – Heighway family connection

I am proud that we have a family link to both the Bartlam family and of course the 'Pig on the wall' postcard. My mother was Alma Marion Heighway (née Masters) and her mother was Aunty Kath's sister Elaine Annie Masters (née Watts). At the age of 15 years mom travelled from Cornwall to live with Aunty Kath and Charles at 72 Court Street, but she had only been there for 10 days when Charles died. My mother stayed on to look after Aunty Kath and Charles and Kathleen's son Christopher and it was here in Madeley that she later met and married my father Archie Heighway. They produced twins, Alan (myself) and Ann and later a further daughter Marilyn who were all born while we lived at 47 Station Road, Madeley, before we moved to 6 Anstice Road in 1962.

The photographers' studio was still running until the around the late 1940s, but now in a room inside the house, while Aunty Kath had

Charles Bartlam on the right with W. Hawkins, J. Jones and Ben Briscoe

Charles Bartlam is the second on the left. The others are not known

Kathleen Bartlam with son Christopher and Alma Masters

Three studio photographs of Alma Heighway (née Masters), on the left with Christopher and in the centre with her husband Archie Heighway

Three studio portraits of Christopher Bartlam, that in the middle with his mother, Kathleen

Christopher Bartlam

also started selling quality jewellery until she later converted the studio into a sweet shop which is how I remember it.

The saving of the 2,500 black and white negatives from being thrown into a rubbish skip in 2006, has given us an wonderful insight into how many Madeley people actually had portraits taken at the Bartlams' studio. Shelagh Lewis contacted me immediately after hearing about the negatives and the Bartlam project was born.

We have had a major task in scanning all these negatives and this work was undertaken initially by me and local historian Pete Wilson and his wife Jenny who volunteered to help

Christopher Bartlam
with Alan (left) and Ann Heighway

me, and to whom I am extremely grateful. It took us two years to complete this process and the Awards for All grant then covered another nine months of professional scanning at Shropshire Archives, and the setting up of a website (created by Andy Craddock of ABC Web Design). With the help of many people it has been possible to name nearly 600 of the portraits saved, all of which are included and named in this book.

We know that many of their negatives have been destroyed, but those saved have now been donated to Shropshire Archives in Shrewsbury.

Alma Heighway with Yvonne Harris (née Masters) on the right
and twins Alan (the author of this book) and Ann Heighway

Surely we can now put Charles and Kath Bartlam high on the list of people whose names should be remembered for their photographic contribution and services to Madeley and Shropshire.

To complete my own personal tribute — with the aid of the lottery grant, we have finally been able to raise a headstone at their previously unmarked grave in St Michael's Churchyard, and, with the aid of modern laser technology, the new headstone bears a copy of the 'Pig on the wall' postcard permanently etched onto it. I feel sure that Charles and Kath Bartlam would have been as proud of it as I am.

Alan Heighway, April 2010

Right: Philip and Elizabeth Heighway. Philip, cousin to Archie Heighway (my father), was a long-serving councillor on Wrekin District Council, of which he became chairman

'Gran' Bertha Beatrice Heighway who ran a groceries shop at 88 Price Street Madeley until she closed it at the age of 87. She died just two days off her 89th birthday

Marilyn, my youngest sister, in the Court Street garden

Elaine Annie Masters (née Watts), Kathleen Bartlam's sister and mother of Alma

Beryl Masters, sister to Alma Heighway (née Masters)

May Rixom (left) and Dorothy (Doll) Heighway, my father Archie Heighway's sisters

The wedding of Joe Holland and Dorothy Heighway, my father's sister. On the left are Jean Groves and Les Rixom, on the right Archie Heighway and May Rixom. Seated is Alma Heighway. Some years later Joe, Les, Doll and May motorcycled to Barmouth where they saw a boat trip being rolled over by the sea. Joe died trying to rescue one of the occupants

Kath Bartlam and Alice Woodfin from Walsall stand beside an Austin Seven, Chummy, of 1928, whilst Alice's partner is beside a BSA 3-wheeler c.1934

Grandad Thomas and Gran Bertha Beatrice Heighway with sons Thomas and probably Stephen. Stephen was accidentally hanged at the age of 12 while making a swing

Archie and Alma Heighway, Bessie and John Masters

Yvonne Harris (née Masters) (left) with her friend Jean Evans

Right: This photograph, taken towards the end of the studio era, shows some of the Masters' children when visiting their Aunty Kath (Bartlam)

Outdoor events, teams and places

Although most of the surviving Bartlam images are conventional studio portraits or wedding groups a small number relate to a wider range of subjects. Some illustrate well-known local sites such as Buildwas Abbey but most relate to the social and cultural activities for which Madeley was justly famous.

Madeley Miners Football Team on the steps of Anstice Memorial Club
Standing (left to right) Mr Taylor, ?, ?, Dennis Beech, Harry Beech (goalkeeper), Jeff Brittland, ?, ?
Middle row: Sid Oliver, Derrick Mullard, Clive Wilde
Front row: Keith Reading, Ken Aldred, Alan Cowdell, Harry (Tich) Hodgson, ?

Madeley Football Team 1948-49
Back row (left to right): ?, Jeff Brittland, ?
Middle row (left to right): Denis Harding, Derek Mullard, 'Dicky' Wilde, Alan Welch, Alan Cowdell

Madeley Football Team (undated)
Back row (left to right): John Price, Derek Mullard, Alan Cowdell
Middle row: Brian Jones, John Hardwick, David Whilby
Front row: Gordon Hatton, John Smart, 'Dicky' Wilde, Ray Gough, Robbie/John Halton

Sports teams were always well-supported in the town and, as well as the football teams depicted here, there was a thriving cricket team and even a quoits team which supplied the 1901 all-England champion!

Fred Whiteley Band
Back row (left to right): Albert Tarrant, Fred Gittings,
Inky Phillips (Albert), Fred Whiteley, Ron France, Billy Harper
Front row: Eric Medley, Ted Baldwin (Dawley),
Albert Gittings, Jimmy Williams

Madeley's bands were renowned throughout the West Midlands and were much in demand for the many events which took place throughout the year. Fêtes, often involving tableaux and plays as well as processions, were organised by the churches and by uniform groups but the highlight of Madeley's social calendar was the annual carnival which took place every year between 1902 and 1956 apart from a break during the Second World War. The carnival always took

Madeley Town Brass Band

place on a Saturday afternoon in late August and commenced with the crowning of the Carnival Queen at 2pm on the steps of 'the Anstice'. The rest of the afternoon was taken up with a procession of decorated floats as well as displays, demonstrations and competitions and the day rounded off with a torchlight procession and a selection of tunes from a local band. The various fancy dress competitions were always well-supported and some of the most eye-catching of the Bartlam images are those of the costumed entrants.

The carnivals were attended by groups and individuals from all over the area including dance troupes and demonstrators from as far afield as Stoke-on-Trent and the Birmingham area. Their success is perhaps best demonstrated by the fact that it was sometimes possible to attract national celebrities, such as Music Hall star Nellie Wallace and the American harmonica player Larry Adler to open the day's proceedings.

Madeley Carnival Female Group

Madeley Carnival Male Group

Tom Cookson, winner of the first prize in the 1926 carnival

Madeley Rectory Gardens Church Play: The Bribe

Madeley Rectory Gardens Church Play: The Three Fishers

Madeley Rectory Gardens Church Play:
Sheba

Madeley Church Garden Party:
Romany Rosa

Coalbrookdale Church Festival

Coalbrookdale parade (soldiers returning
from the second Boer War)

Buildwas Abbey

Farley, Church Street. This was probably one of the first bungalows built in Madeley and was constructed in the 1930s by local builders Broome and Poole. It was built for the Trevor sisters of Much Wenlock (one of whom is probably the lady standing by the porch in the photograph. It was later sold to Telford Development Corporation and then sold on to Tom and Hazel Fowler. Their son, Rob, (for many years a church organist) still lives there today

Studio Photographs

Mrs Dorothy Aldred and Ruth

Vic and Lydia Allen (née York) & Peter

Lydia Allen

Charles Henry Anson and son John (Jack)

Joyce Arden

Cissie Armstrong

Frances Bagley

Noel Bagnall

Doreen Bailey

Jack Bailey and Ida George

John Bailey and Marie George

Minnie Bailey

Miss Bailey

Sarah Bailey and Pat

Alf Barber

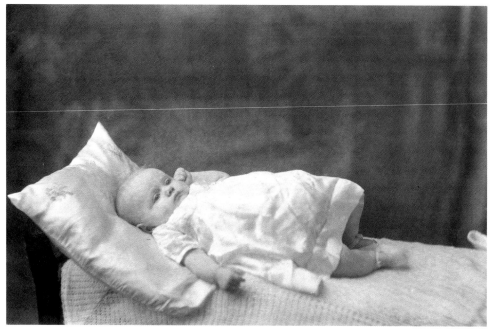

Ann Barker (now Newbrook)

Jean and Mary Barnett

Mr Barnett

Jean Barton and Sheila Booth

Marjorie Bebbington, John Turner,
Hilda Hicks & baby

Mrs Beech with Valerie and Alan

Cllr Edward Bennett

Mayoress Mrs E. Bennett

Mrs Bethell

Audrey Bickerton

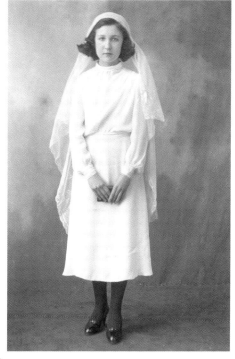

Florrie Biggs

Bill and Florrie Biggs

Florrie Biggs with Marjorie (standing)
and Betty

Kathleen Biggs

Mary Birch

Diane, Mary and Kathleen Blocksidge

Dennis Boden

Dora Boden (née Oliver) and baby

Enoch Boden

Harry Lawrence Walter Boden and Emily Olive Clarke

Emily Olive Boden (née Clarke)
and baby

Emily Olive Boden (née Clarke)

Evelyn Boden

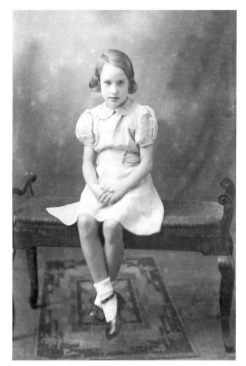

Gwen Boden

Jean Boden

Mary Boden

Joan Boden

Molly Boden

Phyllis Boden
and Clara (Clare) Catherine Drury

Phyllis Boden

Thelma Boden

Thelma Boden

Doris Booth

Doris Booth

John William Booth

Tom Booth

Vera Booth

Mayor Fred Bostock
and Mayoress Mrs Bostock

Fred Bostock

Mayoress Mrs Bostock

Joan, Winnie and Alfred Bowdler

Joan & Winnie Bowdler

Lucy Bowdler

Doug Bradburn and David Edwards

Joan Bradburn and baby

Lily Branson

Grace and Mac Bridgewater

Margaret Bromley

Harry Briscoe

Maurice and Ivor Brown

Peter Brown

Celia Bruce

Jack Brunt

Jean Brunt

Jean Brunt & family

John Bugler and Joan Yates

Valerie Bullock (Mrs Margerrison)

Don Bunting

Dorothy Burgess

Jack Butcher

Pat Carter

Verity Cartwright and sister

Floss Cashmore

John Arthur Cashmore

John Gordon Cashmore

Olive Cheshire

Phyllis Cheshire

David Childs,
son of Jack and Vera Childs

Eileen Clark (née Groves)

George Clarke and Eileen Groves

Joe Clarke and son Terry

Phyllis Clarke

Wendy Coldicott

Lillian Colley and family

Lillian Colley (née Wilkes)

Rose Colley

Walter (Watty) Colley

Denis and Mary Corrigan

Bob Cowdell and Scout group including Jeff Chidlow, Ron Lycett,
Maurice Miller and Ken Newbrook

Walter Currell

Stoker William Currell

Crabtree family

Joan Darlington and baby

Joan Darlington

Graham and Brian Davies

Joyce Davies and friend

Ada Davis and twins

Sheila Davies

Edward Arthur and Edna May Dearing

Grace Dodd

May Dodd

Lillian Dodd

Mabel Dodd (née Beddoes) and John and Rob Walton

Miss Dodd

Miss Dodd

Rosie Dodd

Laurence Dorricott

Clara (Clare) Catherine Drury

Mr Duckett

Mrs Dudley with Kathleen or Eileen

David Edwards

Elsie Edwards

Frank Arthur Edwards

Sandy Edwards

Elsie Elcock

Lillian Elcock (née Boden)

Ron or Don Elcock

Nellie Elcock

Nellie Elcock
and Phyllis Heath (Naylor)

Doris and Nora Embury

Nora Embrey

Nora Embrey

Bill Evans   Carol Evans

Gordon Evans

Ike, Billy and Tom Evans

Maureen Evans

Shirley and June Evans

Mrs Evans and Ralph

Tom Evans

Evans family

Eunice Farlow

Veronica Faulkner

Mr Faulkner and son Ron

Mrs Daisy Ferrington and Keith

Rene Finney

Elizabeth (Lizzie) Fletcher

Harry Fletcher

Harry Fletcher

Some of Harry Fletcher's trophies

William Stanley Foster

Connie Francis

Ethel Franks

Ethel Franks and husband

Fanny Gainham and Iris

Iris Gainham

Mr and Mrs Harry Gainham

Pat Gainham

Mrs Lindan Gainham and David

Lindan Gainham

Wharton Gainham

Jean Garbett

Annie and Doris George

Doris George

Mrs George and Doris

Doris George (née Plant)

Geoff George

Geoff, Doris and Judith George

Edith George

Phyllis George

Ida George

Marie George

Marie George

Richard Thomas and Emily May
George with granddaughter Marie

Freda Godbert

Joan Godbert

Sheila Godbert

Jean Good

Joan Goodwin

Margery Goodwin

Roy Goodwin

Joe and Louie Gough

Vera Gough

Joyce Gravenor

Florence Griffiths and (right) with daughter Shirley and granddaughter
Christine Rushton (seated)

Connie and George Griffiths
(brother and sister)

George, Connie (in hat), Thelma
and Shirley Griffiths (child)

Dinah Groves

Greta Groves

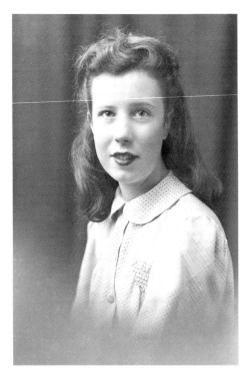

Greta Groves

Jean Groves

Jean, Greta and Peter Groves

Miss Groves (teacher)

Mrs Hack and Roger

Dorothy Hailey

Annie Haines

Flossie Hale

Flossie Hale and Harry Davies

Mrs Hall

Nancy Hall

Charlie Hardman

Vera Hardman

Amy Harper

Dora Harper

Olive Harper

Diane and David Harrington

Kathleen Harrington

Connie Harris

Dolly Harris and Nancy Brown

Joan Harris

Marian Harris

Mrs Harris

Walter Harris and Lucy Jones

Nancy Harris

Phyllis Harris

Joan Harrison

Lily Harrison

Marjorie Harrison

Lucy, Ellen Haseley
with Gillian and Philip

Norman Hassall and Florrie Edwards

Tom Haughton

George and Florence Haynes
and son Kenneth

Jack Haynes and Alice Skitt

Mr Haynes and Joan Haynes

Phyllis Heath

Graham Heighway

Kate Heighway

Joyce Heighway

Nellie Heighway

Helliwell sisters

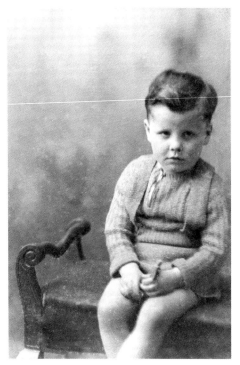

Michael Helliwell

Lillian Helliwell and cousin Aline Baker

Cyril Hickman and Mabel Gough

Marjorie Hicks

Muriel Higginson

Phyllis Higginson

Les and Cecilia Higgs
with Janet and Carol

John and Edith Hill

Sid Hill

Phyllis Hill

Tom Howells

Eileen Humphries

Eileen Humphries-Watson

Joan Hurdley

Zavina Hurdley

Geoffrey Jackson

Mary Jackson (née Jones)

Donald William Jeffereys

Alec Jeffrey

Mr Jenks

Nancy Jenks

Ray Jenks

Patricia Jervis

Sheila Jesse

Lena Johnson

Albert Jones

Alf Jones

Betty Jones

Billy Jones (civilian) and friend

Dorothy Jones

Ella Jones

Glenys and Alan Jones

Laurence Jones

Glenys Jones

Joan Jones (Yorke)

Lucy Jones (married Walter Harris)
and sister

Margaret, Terry and Ivor Jones

Margery Jones

Marianne and Pauline Jones

Miss Jones

Mary Jones

Mary Jones

Mr Jones

Nellie Jones

Mrs Jones and Ella

Mrs Jones and Brian

Jones sisters

Topsy Jones (née Yeomans)

Topsy Jones and family

Rene Jones

Jones children

V. Jones

Vera Jones

Etta Keay

Mary Kelsey

Joan Kelsey

Rene Kelsey

Alice Maud Knight

The Lewis children

Miss Lewis

Lily Lister

Albert Lloyd

Annie Lloyd (née Hodgson)

Bert Lloyd

Betty Lloyd (née Harper)
and Lorraine ('Poppy')

Doreen Ann Lloyd

Edna Lloyd

Lilly Lloyd

Les Lloyd

Mary Lloyd, Lilian Lloyd, Joan Lloyd, Joan Sambrook and Kath Sambrook

Mary Lloyd

Mrs Lloyd with twins and Joan

Miss Lloyd

Mr Lloyd

Edith Locklin

Edith Lowe

Jean Lycett

Ron Lycett and right (standing) with two other scouts

Dora Mannering with Peter and Wendy

Dora Mannering with Peter and Wendy

Pam Melvin

Marian Meredith

Ernie Merrick

Maurice Miller

Mrs Miller (or Mrs Taylor) and Clare

Harold Minton

Jean Minton

Miss Minton (teacher)

Mr Moore (Rob)

Pat and Eileen Morgan with baby

Jean Mullard

Roland Naylor and Phyllis (née Heath)

Greta Newbrook

Bill Noble

Dorothy Noble

Mary Northall

Nellie Oakes

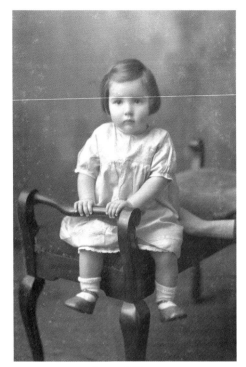

Janet Oliver

Stuart Oliver

Bill Osbourne

Edith Oakley

Albert Owen and friend

Ann and David Owen

Dorothy Paisley

Marion Owen

Mrs K. Parton and Kenny

Peter Parton

Mrs Parton with Betty, Peter and Kenny

Vera Payne

Herbie Payne & Laura (Girlie)

Herbie Payne (sitting) and friend

Herbie Payne and Laura (Girlie)

Herbie Payne

Bob and Mary Pearce

Dorothy Pearce

Arthur Pemberton and friend

May Perkins

George Perks

Mr and Mrs George Perks

Walter Perks

Mr Phillpott

Mrs Phillpott

William John (Jack) Phillpott

Doris Plant

Mrs Polres and baby

Doreen and Olive Poole

Phillip John Ernest Poole

Joan Pope

Rose and Kenneth Pooler

Eileen Powell

Enoch and Gertie Price

Miss Price

Gwilym Pugh and Iris Gainham

Mrs Reynolds and baby

Mr Richards

Betty Rickers

Betty Rickers and brother

Doris Roberts

Eileen Sylvia Roberts

Gertrude Ivy Roberts

Joan Roberts

Thomas Raymond Roberts

Maud Roberts on the right,
with Sally and Hilda Jones

Valerie Rowe

Miss J.M. Rowley

Albert Russell

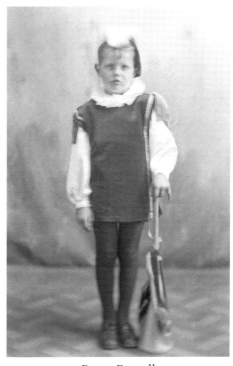

Barry Russell

Judy Russell

Kathleen Russell

Madge and John Russell

Walter Russell

Annie Sambrook (née Lloyd)

Mrs Sambrook with Eileen, Joan,
Kathleen and Annie

Joan and Kath Sambrook

Mrs Joan Sambrook and children

Tommy Sambrook

Ron Saunders

George and Winnie Scoltock

Mrs Nelly Sharrock and Alan

Irene Shenton

George Shepherd,
Tom Booth and Mr Booth

Bob Shepherd and Kath Harper

Mabel Shepherd

Mary Shepherd

Mary Shepherd

Mary Shepherd

Mary Shepherd

Norman Simpson

Harry Skeats

Marion and Margaret Skeet

Alice Skitt

Derek Skitt

Mary Skitt

Doris Slack

Jack Smart

Jack Smart

Les and Cynthia Smith

Norma Smith

Joan Smout   Jean Standell (née Davis)

Jean Stephan

Jim Stevenson

Lizzie Stewart

Jack (Nip) Stokes

Florence Sumnall, Emily Deakin,
Lily Evans and baby

Ron and Sheila Swift

Dawn Tart

Lillian Taylor (née Seabury)

Sidney Thomas

May Thompson

Frank & Rene Thompson with Barbara

Barbara Thompson

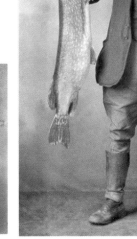

G. Thorne and his pike

Bert Timmins

Florrie Timmins

Joan Tomkinson and Pam Melvin

Noel Tomkinson

Joan and Mary Tompkinson

Norman Tonks

Brenda Tranter

Phyllis Tristham and Dennis

Joan or Shelagh Vickers

Lily Walton with John, Tony and Rob

Lily Walton and Tony

John and Rob Walton

Tony, Rob and John Walton

Norman and Mary Walton

Lily Walton

Jeanette and Carol Ward

Jack and Phyllis Whale

Eileen and Nancy Webb

Bernard, Eileen, Maureen and Jeff Webb

David, Jeanette and Patricia Whiteley

Millie Whiteley

Patricia Whiteley

Patricia and Jeanette Whiteley

Beryl Wilde

Chris Wilde

Chris Wilde

Mr and Mrs Wilde with Shirley

Shirley Wilde

Shirley Wilde (as bridesmaid)

James William Wilkes

Mr Wilkes

Vera Wilkes

Miss Wilkinson (Groves)

Jack and Grace Williams with son Michael

Michael Williams

Ida Wilton

Josephine Withers (née Reece)

Emma (Emmy) Woodman
with Amelia, Bill, Thomas and Daisy

Edna, Iris and Eileen Workman

Edna Workman

George Workman

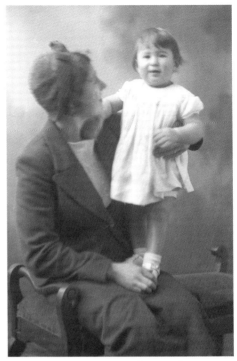

Mrs Wright and Dorothy

Dorothy Wright

Dorothy Wright

John and Nellie Wycherley

Violet Yates

Judith York

Harold Yorke

Tommy Yorke

Wedding Photographs

Samuel Birch and Kathleen Leighton

John Bugler and Joan Yates

Denis and Mary Corrigan

Joan Darlington

Les Davey and Joan Harrison

Standing, left to right: Rene Jones (née Kelsey), Will Plant, Geoff George, Doris Plant, Dennis Jones, Mary Kelsey. Sitting: Joan Kelsey, Kathleen Kelsey

Joe Gibbons and Phyllis Harris

Left to right: May Rowley (née Gough), Cis Gough, Lucy Lloyd (née Gough), Louie Gough,
Joe Gough, Billy Owen, Mabel Hickman (née Gough), ?, Mrs Gough, Billy Gough,
with the small girls in front: Hazel Jones and Veronica Gough

Mr and Mrs Don Harper (bridesmaid Amy)

Jack Haynes and Alice Skitt

Cyril and Mabel Hickman

Billy Hill and May Johnson

Tommy Howells and Grace Jones

Eric Jenkinson and Mary Drury

Edward Maiden and Eileen McMahon

Teddy Millward and Hilda Jackson

Jean Minton

Cyril Mortimer and Mary Skitt

Matthew Owen and Kathleen Boden

Enoch and Gertie Price

Back row, left to right: Frank Anson, Jack Anson, George Pritchard, Florrie Anson, Charlie Anson, Bert Anson, Mona Anson. Front row: ?, Georgina Cartwright, Elsie Forgham

Back row: Michael Browning, G.T. Pugh, Gwilym Pugh, Iris Gainham, George Gainham
Front row: Ivy Pugh, Hilda Pugh, Pat Gainham, Faye Gainham, Joyce Gainham

Alf Sambrook and Lilly Harrison

George and Winnie Scoltock

Bob Shepherd and Kath Harper

Les Smith and Cynthia Jones

Ron and Sheila Swift

Ted White and Miss Branson

John and Nellie Wycherley

John and Nellie Wycherley
Amongst the party are: Tom Baggot (standing fourth from right), Jim Baggot (standing third from right), Annie (standing second from right), Aunty Annie from Liverpool (seated front row second from left), Mrs Baggot (seated next to groom) and Alice Pillar (seated next to bride)

Index